About this Book

Ronnie's Great Idea is a story about the life and work of Dr. Ronald L. Mallett. Dr. Mallett is an African American physicist who is one of the world leaders in time travel research. He currently works at the University of Connecticut and has a patent on a time travel machine. Dr. Mallett's interest in time travel began as a child shortly after his father died. Learning about time travel through fiction, Ronald thought that by building a time machine he might be able to travel back in time and save his father's life. What began as a childhood fantasy grew into his life's work.

As a biographical fiction, *Ronnie's Great Idea* presents key events events in Dr. Mallett's life through a fictionalized story. The book begins with Ronald as a young child and ends with him as a university professor. The story describes challenges faced by the main character. In the face of these challenges, it is his drive to create a time machine and the support of his family that help him to persist.

Ronnie's Great Idea is especially powerful for children of African descent. Stories like that of Dr. Mallett are too little known. It is difficult to see the power and potential we have as a race when our heroes are not shown and their stories are not told. *Ronnie's Great Idea* is a powerful departure from the norm. It is a valuable resource for Black children and adults alike.

As a Level 4 Reader, *Ronnie's Great Idea* introduces children to chapters, presents challenging themes, and offers great new vocabulary words. This text is a powerful learning resource for parents and teachers, and great fun for children!

1

D1517799

Sankoré Institute

11715 Fox Road
Suite 400-173
Indianapolis, IN 46236

© 2016 by Jomo W. Mutegi, Ph.D.

Visit our web site at www.JomoMutegi.com

ISBN-13: 978-0-9789415-8-1

Printed in the United States of America

First Printing by Sankoré Institute: September 2016

To Master Andric and Miss Alaira Moultrie

Fear no forest because it is dense.

~ African Proverb

SI Leveled Readers

1	**E**arly Readers . These books are for beginning readers. They feature simple words, picture clues, and fewer vocabulary words. Here children continue their love of reading!
2	**D**eveloping Readers. These books are for shared reading. They feature advanced words, increased dialogue, and fewer vocabulary words. These books are both challenging and fun!
3	**I**ndependent Readers. These books are for newly independent readers. They feature longer sentences, short paragraphs, and an increasing number of vocabulary words. Children experience the joy and satisfaction of independence with these books!
4	**A**dvanced Readers. These books are for advanced readers. They introduce children to chapters, they present challenging themes, and they offer great new vocabulary words. Children are off and running with these books!

Ronnie's Great Idea

Chapter One
Ronnie's Grand Plan

Ever since the funeral, Ronnie read all the time. Today, Ronnie was reading quietly in his room. He had been reading all day. He ate no breakfast. He ate no lunch. All he had eaten today was a cooked bologna sandwich. His mother, Dorothy, made him eat at least that much for dinner.

He was reading a book titled *Time Machine*. He loved it! Not because it was a great book, but because while reading it, he came up with his Great Idea! He would build a time machine of his own so that he could travel back in time and save his father's life.

As Ronnie thought about his Great Idea, he remembered back to when he was very young. He remembered how his father, Boyd, would come home after working all day. Although Boyd would be tired, he always made time for the entire family: Dorothy, Ronnie, Ronnie's younger brothers Keith and Jason, and especially Ronnie's baby sister Eve.

After eating dinner together, Dorothy would clean up while the younger children would play. Boyd would pull Ronnie aside and use an old television to teach Ronnie something new about electronics. When the children went to bed, Boyd would spend time with Dorothy. Ronald sometimes heard them whispering on the couch. Dorothy always spoke kindly and said nice things about her husband. Ronnie really missed his father.

One Saturday morning, after he finished reading *Time Machine*, Ronnie decided that he was ready to build a time machine of his very own. He read portions of the book that described the time machine. He looked at pictures in the book that showed the time machine. Ronnie then made a list of things he would need: string, large cardboard boxes, glue, tape, the blade of a house fan, a steering wheel, and of course an old clock.

Ronnie spent the entire day reading the book, examining pictures, drawing diagrams, and building the machine. ...reading, examining, drawing and building. ...reading, examining, drawing and building. He didn't watch TV. He didn't go out to play. He didn't eat. He only stopped when it was time to sleep.

Then Sunday morning he woke, washed, and went back to work. Finally, just before dinner on Sunday evening he finished. He gathered his mother, brothers, and sister and showed them his creation. He did not tell them his Great Idea. That would be a surprise. But they were all very excited by his creation.

His mother, Dorothy, beamed with pride and she made an especially good dinner. Dinner was filled with chatter about Ronnie's creation, and near the end, Dorothy surprised everyone with a peach cobbler and ice cream dessert. It was everyone's favorite!

The next day Ronnie woke full of hope and excitement. At school, he invited some of his friends to come see his special surprise. At home that day, before Dorothy returned from work, Ronnie unveiled his time machine for his friends.

"What is it?" one of them asked.
"It's a time machine," Ronnie responded proudly. "I built it. Now I'm going to go back in time and save my father." With that, Ronnie sat in the front of his machine. He reached forward to adjust the clock.

He reached back to flip the switch on the fan blade. But nothing happened. The clock simply flashed at Ronnie and the fan blew dust throughout the room. As Ronnie sat there puzzled the boys began to snicker. When he turned the fan speed up to a higher setting, they began to laugh aloud. Ronnie tapped the clock, and they began to laugh uncontrollably. Ronnie fumed with anger. He jumped off of his machine and sent the boys out of his house.

14

Ronnie sulked through the entire dinner that evening. Neither Dorothy, nor Jason, nor Keith, nor Eve said anything. Just as Ronnie was getting up to leave the table, Dorothy rubbed his back and whispered to him, "It's still a Great Idea. Keep at it. You will make it work one day."

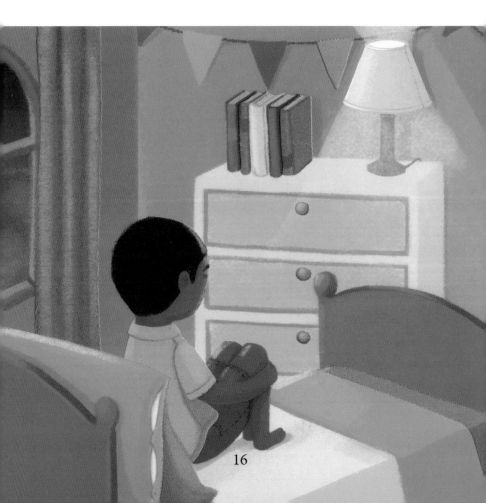

Before going to bed that night Keith came to Ronnie's room with a painting of Ronnie's time machine. Standing next to it were Ronnie and Boyd. They had their hands raised and they were wearing big smiles. Ronnie smiled at his little brother and gave him a hug. When Ronnie went to bed he realized that he could only trust his Great Idea to people who were special to him. For all others, it must be a Great Secret!

That night, as Ronnie lay in bed, he remembered the many things his father taught him. Boyd taught Ronnie about electrons, which he called "tiny workers." He explained to Ronnie that these tiny workers gave televisions their power. They also powered other things like clocks, toasters, and light bulbs. His father believed that these tiny workers would be the power source of the future.

Ronnie remembered his father telling him that one day Ronnie would need to learn more about electricity and electronics. As Ronnie slept that night he was no longer angry. He slept with the calm that comes from the gentle touch of a loving mother, the caring gesture of a loving brother, and the wise instruction of a loving father.

The next morning before going to school Ronnie told his mother that he needed to learn more about electricity to make his time machine work. "Mom, how can I learn about electricity?"

"I suppose the best place to start is at the library!" She replied.

That evening Dorothy took Ronnie and the whole gang to the library. Everyone brought back one or two books that struck them as interesting -- except for Ronnie. Ronnie had a grocer's bag full of books on electricity.

Over the next few weeks, Ronnie would pour over these books, learning everything he could about electricity. When he had gone through these, he would return to the library to get another load and start again.

Chapter Two
The Family's Big Move

Even in his absence, Boyd Mallett provided his family with so much. Ronnie remembered his father's wisdom and advice. Keith and Jason were always reminded of his firm and loving guidance. Eve admired his strength. Dorothy, even now, felt his protection and the security he provided. What he was not able to provide in his absence was the daily sustenance that the family needed. This was a difficult time for Dorothy as she struggled to provide good clothes and food in her husband's absence.

Seeing this, Dorothy's father sent for the family to move to Pennsylvania where he could help them through this difficult time.

When he heard the news, Ronnie was both excited and nervous. He was excited because he loved spending time with his grandpa

and grandma. He was nervous because he was not sure that he could take his books with him. Before he was able to ask, Dorothy smiled at him and said, "Of course there will be plenty of room for your library..." then turning to Keith she added, "...and your art studio."

Grandma & Granddad

Everyone really loved being in Pennsylvania. Grandma always gave great hugs and kisses, Grandpa always told great stories, and absolutely everyone loved the great food! It seemed, however, that not everyone loved the Malletts.

One day Ronnie was walking with his mother to the grocery store. On their way back there was a group of boys about Ronnie's age who looked like trouble. As Ronnie and his mother passed the boys, Dorothy smiled politely and said, "Good afternoon, boys."

A few moments later Ronnie heard one of the boys call out, a racial slur.[*]

Ronnie felt his heart race. He stopped
cold in his tracks and spun around and headed
straight towards the group of boys. He wasn't
sure which boy made the comment, but he
walked up to the boy who seemed to be in
charge. Without a word Ronnie pulled back
his fist and hit him in the eye. As the boy fell,
Ronnie leapt on him and continued hitting him
until he stopped struggling.

All of the other boys and Dorothy simply
watched. They were stunned and didn't know
what to do. Ronnie got up and walked slowly
back towards his mother. He had fought and
messed up his clothes. He just knew that he
was going to be punished.

As they walked back towards the house neither Ronnie nor Dorothy said anything for a very long time. Ronnie never looked away from his feet. After some time he looked up at his mother and said softly, "I'm sorry."

Dorothy smiled and rubbed his back gently, "Ronnie, don't be sorry. Self-respect is the foundation of justice. Your father taught me that."

Dorothy never said it directly, but Ronnie knew that she was proud of him. He also knew that his father would have been proud. The two never spoke of the event again, but Ronnie never forgot what his mother had said, "Self-respect is the foundation of justice."

Chapter Three
The Date That Never Was

As Ronald grew older he was very shy. Throughout high school, he enjoyed reading and studying, especially mathematics and physics. And Ronald never lost sight of his goal of building the time machine.

Sometimes on Saturdays Ronald would spend the entire day with his grandfather building and fixing things around the house. During these times his grandfather would caution him not to isolate himself. "Friendship is very important in life," he would say.

As Ronald thought long and hard about what his grandfather said, he remembered back to when he was very young. He remembered that when all the kids were put to bed he would sneak out and watch his parents from around the corner.

He remembered how his father, Boyd, would put a record on the old record player, and he would slowly dance with his mother for what seemed like hours. He remembered how excited his mother would be. She was all smiles and giggles dancing on that living room floor.

Ronald realized that he wanted a wife and children one day. He wanted to provide them all of the joy that his own father had provided. There was a young lady in his physics class that caught his eye. Her name was Virginia. Virginia was the most beautiful girl that he had known. She reminded him of Dorothy Dandridge.

Sometimes when Ronald would come to class, Virginia would save him a seat next to hers. In return, Ronald would always offer to carry Virginia's books to her next class. Virginia was very happy and excited about her growing friendship with Ronald. She hoped that he would ask her to the prom.

One day, a very jealous girl that ate lunch with Virginia fibbed. She told Virginia that Ronald had asked someone else to the prom. After that, Virginia was very embarrassed. She never again saved seats for Ronald in class.

Ronald was heartbroken. He couldn't figure out what he had done to upset Virginia. He wanted to ask her to the prom, but he thought she no longer liked him. Ronald finished the rest of his time in high school without ever going on a date or even showing interest in another girl.

Chapter Four
Ronald's Great Disappointment

After high school, many of the white kids went to college. College was very expensive. Even though many of the Black students wanted to go to college, it was not affordable. So the Black students often went right to work.

Ronald thought long and hard about going to college so that he could learn more physics and mathematics. He knew that going to college would be the best way to learn what he needed in order to build his time machine.

An older friend of the family told Ronald
that if he went to the military for four years,
then he could pay for college with the money
he earned. So Ronald signed up for the United
States Air Force.

Ronald often thought about Virginia. It made him very sad that they were never able to get to know one another better. Being in the military gave a Ronald a chance to try to get over the sadness he felt. He thought that he would really work hard to make friends with the other airmen and to possibly even meet a nice lady.

One day Ronald and some of the other airmen had time away from the base. They decided to go into the local town, have dinner, and watch a movie. As they went into the restaurant, a group of whites from the town surrounded Ronnie. They began cursing at him and yelling insults.

A fat, greasy man wearing a soiled apron came out from the kitchen and told Ronald to leave saying, "We don't serve your kind here, boy!"

Ronald looked at his friends hoping for some support. Most of them looked away without saying anything. Finally, one of the soldiers looked at Ronnie and said, "Just head back to base, Ron. We'll be back soon."

Ronald was livid! He had to walk back 8 miles to the base because the airman who drove a car stayed at the restaurant. He could not believe that none of the others would speak or act in his defense. He could not believe that they would stay and eat in that restaurant after he had been treated so badly.

On this long walk back to the base Ronald had a lot of time to think. In that time he realized that those soldiers were not really his friends. Friends do not treat you badly. He also realized that he had started getting away from his goal of building a time machine. "You can't build a time machine eating in a greasy restaurant with uncivilized people," he thought. At that, Ronald decided that he would focus even more on his time machine.

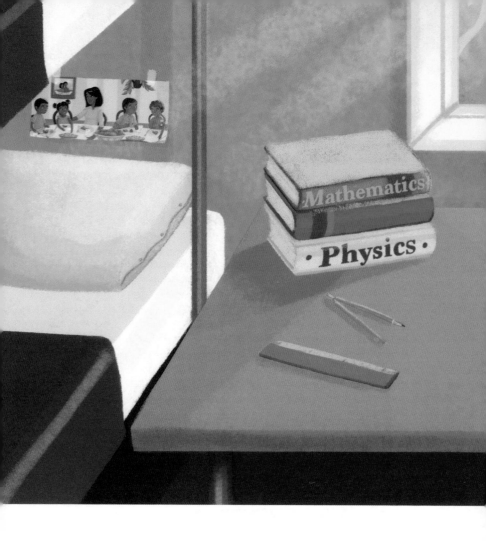

At his first opportunity, Ronald did what he had been doing for years. He went to the nearest library and he borrowed as many books as he could carry in one trip. Now he was reading books that were very complicated to understand. In fact, there were some that he did not understand. He simply read them anyway.

He noticed symbols in mathematics books that he had never seen before. He wondered, "How can I teach myself the meaning of these symbols?" Mathematics is like a different language. He noticed words in physics books that he had never heard before. He wondered, "How can I teach myself the meaning of these words?" Physics is like a different language.

Even though Ronald thought that he couldn't understand some of the books, his effort paid off. He learned more than he thought. He began to see the same words and symbols over and over again. He began to have an idea of what they meant. For four years, Ronald immersed himself in his books. He never thought about trying to be friends with the other soldiers. His only dream was to build a time machine and to have Virginia by his side when he did it.

Elijah Muhammad

Malcolm X

Robert F. Williams

Black Panthers

Dedan Kimathi

Chapter Five
Dr. Mallett's Great Achievement

While in the Air Force, Ronald saved up enough money to pay for college. When he went to college, there were many Black people all over the world fighting for better treatment. Ronald thought about the way he and his mother were insulted by the little boy in Altoona. He thought about the way he was mistreated in the military. He liked these Black people because they would make life better for all Black people.

One day Ronald was approached by two men from the FBI. These men asked Ronnie to spy on the Black college students who were fighting for better treatment. Ronald stood up to the FBI. He refused to help. He told them that he would never work to hurt other Black people.

Ronald finally graduated from college. Everyone was very proud of him, his mother Dorothy, his brothers Keith and Jason, and even his sister Eve. They were so proud of him that they began calling him Dr. Mallett.

After graduating from college, Dr. Mallett went to work for a company that made lasers. He made a lot of money with this job and he also learned a lot about lasers. He liked the company and he liked making a lot of money, but he was still very sad. He was sad because he always thought of Virginia and he wished that she were able to be with him. He was also sad because he really wanted to build a time machine.

Dr. Mallett decided to take matters into his own hands. He left the laser company and took a job working at the University of Connecticut. At the university, he made less money. His main job was to teach classes and to do research. Dr. Mallett could do any type of research that he wanted to do. So, he chose to do research on time travel.

After many years of doing research, Dr. Mallet finally came up with an idea for a time travel machine. But he did not tell anyone. Before sharing his idea, he was going to make sure that it was perfect. This way no one would laugh at his idea.

Dr. Mallett's idea was to build a time travel machine that used lasers to bend space and time. He worked for hours, days, weeks, and months, making sure that his time travel machine would work. Finally, when he was sure it would work, he wrote a paper about his idea. He also got a patent on a blueprint for his time machine. This way no one would steal his idea.

Dr. Mallet now leads a team of scientists who are using his blueprint as a guide to building a real working model of his time travel machine. The young man who once dreamed of building a time machine to save his father's life is now a grown man. Dr. Mallett is still

living today. He is still working as a professor at the University of Connecticut.

    We don't know what the future holds. We don't know whether Dr. Mallett will travel back in time to save his father. We don't know if he will find Virginia or a woman like her and finally have the family that he has always wanted. What we do know is that Dr. Ronald Lawrence Mallett has done more for time travel research than any other physicist living, and we are certain that his father, Boyd Mallett, would be extremely proud of him!

Discussion Topics

Below are a few questions drawn from the book. Some of these questions require simple recall. Others require exploration outside of the text, and a few are designed to encourage discussion and deeper thinking. Use these questions as an opportunity to have rich discussions with your young reader.

1) How and when did Ronald Mallett become interested in time travel?

2) Where was Ronald Mallett born? Locate this city on a map.

*3) Page 26 describes an instance when Ronnie beat up a little boy in Altoona, PA. The boy called Ronnie and his mother, "Uppity Niggers!" Why did Ronnie beat this boy?

4) "Self-Respect is the foundation of justice." What does this quote mean?

5) Why did the FBI approach Dr. Mallett when he was in graduate school?

6) Why did Dr. Mallett leave the laser company?

7) What challenges did Dr. Mallett overcome to be successful?

8) What character traits did Dr. Mallett have that enabled him to be successful?

Growing Our Vocabulary

Ronnie's Great Idea introduces advanced readers to a broad range of new words. If you have read any other Black Kids Read books, you know that vocabulary development is a central feature. There are a number of success markers (such as college graduation, and annual income) that correlate positively with vocabulary. Quite simply, the more words we know, the more likely we are to advance educationally and to earn more money.

By the time children are using Level 4 Readers, they should be able to make sense of new words by using context clues and also by consulting outside sources (such as a dictionary).

Below is a list of new vocabulary words from _Ronnie's Great Idea_ Have your young reader read the book to you. Have your young reader stop upon reading new words. Ask questions to determine how well your young reader understands these words. Where needed, discuss the use of context clues and consult a dictionary for unfamiliar words.

1. Admire	11. Fume	21. Puzzle
2. Affordable	12. Gesture	22. Self-Respect
3. Airmen	13. Grocer	23. Soiled
4. Caution	14. Immerse	24. Sulk
5. Chatter	15. Isolate	25. Sustenance
6. Electronics	16. Leapt	26. Symbol
7. Electrons	17. Portion	27. Time Machine
8. Embarrassed	18. Pour	28. Unveil
9. Examine	19. Power	
10. Fibbed	20. Prom	

About the Author

Jomo W. Mutegi, Ph.D. is a mild-mannered professor by day and a relentless revolutionary by night. As a professor, Dr. Mutegi's area of expertise is science education. He studies the participation of African people in science, technology, engineering, and mathematics (STEM). He received a Bachelor's of Science degree in Chemistry and Biology from Gannon University; and he received a Doctorate in Science Education from Florida State University. He has published numerous manuscripts summarizing his research findings and theoretical arguments. He has taught thousands of prospective and practicing teachers, as well as K-12 students. He has helped to guide the research careers of several very accomplished STEM education researchers.

As a revolutionary, Dr. Mutegi is guided by the counsel of Dr. Amos Wilson who reminds us that, "The function of education is to secure the survival of a people." To this end he has committed himself to creating educational materials aimed at securing the survival of African people. These include curricular materials (e.g. lessons, modules, units, workshops, courses, activities, readers, and books) that can be used in both formal and non-formal settings. Most of these curricular materials focus primarily on STEM subject areas as they are relevant to African people.